REFRAME: THE MAGAZINE FOR PROFESSIONAL HYPNOTISTS

A PUBLICATION OF THE ICBCH, INC.

DR. RICHARD K. NONGARD
EXECUTIVE DIRECTOR

Editor in Chief
CHRISTINA MATTHEWS, LCPC

Associate Editor
RICHARD DAMA, LPC

CONTENTS

01 … From the President's Desk

07 … Integrating Neurolinguistic Programming (NLP) to Improve Communication, Gain Rapport by Christina Matthews, MS MA LCPC CCHI, Editor in Chief

13 … It's Time to Reconsider How You Use Age Regression Approach in Hypnosis by Kelley T. Woods

19 … Cognitive Behavioral Hypnotherapy: The Limbic System by Richard D. Dama, LPC

30 … Faster Tapping as a Useful Technique with Clients by Toni Macri Reiner

35 ... Ideas on Creating Powerful Direct
Suggestions Based on the Hierarchy of Values
(Hierarchy of Criteria) by Leonardo Silvério

41 ... Decreasing Anticipatory Response of Nausea
in Chemotherapy by James Malone

45 ... Pathway to True Healing: How to Heal
Cellular Memories by Patricia Eslava Vessey,
PCC, CHt.

52 ... Bedwetting and the Hypnotist by Seth-
Deborah Roth, RN, CRNA, CCHt

58 ... FREE Weight Loss Hypnosis Script: Four
Sessions to a New Life by Richard Nongard

FROM THE PRESIDENT'S DESK

DR. RICHARD K. NONGARD

I AM EXCITED **about the growth of the ICBCH over the past two years.** All of our growth has been organic as people have sought out affiliation with an organization that truly seeks to serve the community and other professionals. Our ICBCH Train-The-Trainer program has welcomed over 60 new trainers who join our existing network of trainers to offer high quality training both online, offline and in hybrid formats.

One of the big problems in America has been healthcare for self-employed people. Many professional hypnotists have struggled with maintaining a day job just for health insurance, and the ICBCH is committed to finding resources for its members. Our group health care plan meets the needs of self-employed hypnotists (any ICBCH member can access our group plans regardless of employment status. You only need to be an ICBCH member to qualify). Our plans can save you money, and will cover your family members, spouses, children and even any employees you have.

We continue to offer options and resources for professional liability insurance and look forward to the coming months when we can announce a new plan that can help you protect your business. A lot of great things are happening at the ICBCH and this magazine for professional hypnotists is a free resource for members.

Are you passionate about helping other people with professional hypnosis? We are most excited about the **2020 ICBCH Winter HypnoConference** coming up February 17-19, 2020 in Las Vegas. This is the conference to attend if you are passionate about helping others with professional hypnosis. The speakers we select are doing the real work of professional hypnosis. It is not the biggest convention, nor the flashiest, but if you are looking for evidence-based methods of helping people with professional hypnosis, you will want to attend.

The ICBCH is a non-profit educational membership association dedicated to protecting your right to practice professional hypnosis and providing real world benefits that help you to succeed in professional hypnosis. If you are reading this and you are not a member of the ICBCH please join us by either taking an approved training program or joining us through reciprocity if you are certified by another recognized hypnosis organization. You can find the link to join through reciprocity right here: www.hypnotherapyboard.com

Best Wishes,
Dr. Richard Nongard

To access our group healthcare plans, our liability coverage options, register for the 2020 Winter HypnoConference or register for a training, visit our website at: www.hypnotherapyboard.com

The HYPNOSIS CONVENTION for those Passionate about Helping Other People... Clinical Hypnosis Training for Caring Professionals

(ICBCH Continuing Education Hours Provided)

ALL THREE DAYS, ALL SPEAKERS, ONE LOW REGISTRATION RATE!

Karen Hand and Kelley T. Woods
with Keynote by Jason Linette

DAY ONE – All Day Seminar

One Day Intensive "How to Create Hypnosis Workshops for the Public" is included in your 3-day registration!

MONDAY, FEBRUARY 17 | 9:00AM-5:00PM

Karen Hand and Kelley T. Woods are going to help you create outstanding hypnosis workshops and seminars for the public. If you have ever wondered how to use hypnosis in group settings to create interest and referrals to your practice, they have the answers. You will learn what seminars people want to attend, and how to structure and create programs that sell. This is perhaps one of the single best skills you can learn if you want to build a thriving private practice with lots of community referrals. Be a part of this event!

---

25 Expert Level Speakers Sharing the Exact Tools They Use to Create Therapeutic Success

Two full days packed with approved continuing education that will change your client outcomes

TUESDAY AND WEDNESDAY, FEBRUARY 18-19, 2020 | 8AM-6PM EACH DAY

We have hand-picked the highest rated speakers, with the most practical ideas and innovative approaches. We want you to leave this conference not only having had a great time but also maximizing your potential as a passionate hypnotherapist. We record everything, but the video is ONLY available to those who pre-register for the conference. This way, even though you have to make a choice as to which room to attend, you still get them all a few weeks after the conference!

THE NEXT STEP!

Now that you have saved your seat, get your hotel reservations! The Orleans is offering the first 100 to book room nights a special discount (plus mandatory resort fee). The Orleans Hotel and Casino is a landmark hotel in Las Vegas. It is conveniently located near the south end of Las Vegas Blvd. but just off the strip at 4500 W Tropicana Ave in Las Vegas, Nevada. All travel, lodging and meals expenses are the responsibility of attendee and are not included in conference registration/tuition fees.

Questions? Call (702) 418-3332 to Register by Phone or visit HPTI.org to Register Online

INTEGRATING NEUROLINGUISTIC PROGRAMMING (NLP) TO IMPROVE COMMUNICATION, GAIN RAPPORT

CHRISTINA MATTHEWS, MS MA LCPC CCHI, EDITOR IN CHIEF

NEUROLINGUISTIC PROGRAMMING (NLP) began in the mid-1970s. Its originators, Richard Bandler, a mathematician and computer programmer, working with Dr. John Grinder, a linguistics professor, were interested in creating a model to replicate the language patterns and behaviors of highly successful individuals. Three successful people they sought out on their quest were famous hypnotist Dr. Milton Erikson, Dr. Virginia Satir, and Dr. Fritz Perls, who greatly influenced the direction of their research. As the NLP model developed, they began to explain behavior linguistically, creating what are now referred to as metamodels. There is no clear agreement on the number of metamodels that now exist, but today, NLP metamodels the the techniques derived from them are used by advertisers, presidents, salesmen, hypnotherapists, and even everyday people to improve all aspects of their lives. Unfortunately, Bandler and Grinder did not focus on protecting the rights of their research and innovations. Currently, there are countless individuals worldwide who imitate and teach their methods but fail to acknowledge the origin of NLP.

NLP takes years of intensive study to understand and master all its elements, but there are a few basics we can quickly grasp which can help us improve communication and gain rapport with our clients right away. In this article, Subjective Model Favored Internal Representation System (IRS) Sensory Predicates, Body Signals, and Eye-Accessing Cues will be presented.

SUBJECTIVE MODEL FAVORED INTERNAL REPRESENTATION SYSTEM:

Sensory Predicates

According to Bandler, a good therapist should be goal-oriented, have sensory acuity, be flexible, regard client challenges as an opportunity to learn something new, help solve a problem instead of fixing a broken person, be able to develop rapport, have intuitive skills, and be able to understand the way a client interprets his/her world by evaluating the words and behaviors they use that represent their internal reality (internal map or IRS.) The therapist must also realize that no change will take place if the client does not want to change; the client needs to view the problem from a new perspective; and the changes must be motivating and practiced.

Everyone creates a unique internal map based on their own experiences. Maps do not always represent everything available to be experienced and are influenced by neurology, society, and personal beliefs. Personal experiences form likes, dislikes, habits, rules, beliefs, and values. It is important to help the client make the right changes to his or her map and to make the most effective map.

Internal maps or IRS are based on how sensory information is stored. Individuals tend to favor one or two of their five senses [visual, auditory, kinesthetic, olfactory, gustatory.] It is helpful to know which senses are dominant to help make communication most meaningful.

Being able to determine the representational style of a client will help build rapport and effective communication. It is relatively easy to determine what sensory modality the client uses just by paying attention to some cues. The first type of cues are language cues. *Visual clients may say, for example, "I see what you mean," or, "I don't see why this is necessary." Auditory clients may say "My spouse gave me an earful!" A kinesthetic client may say, "I had a gut feeling about this," or "This is unbearable!"*

Another way to determine a client's IRS might be to ask them to tell you about their favorite place. Don't lead their thoughts with any specific directions. Just listen and evaluate the words they use to describe it. This can also give clues to the client's primary sensory modality. Understanding how the client interprets the world should influence how to communicate with the client by mirroring the types of words they use. They will relate more easily and it helps the client feel understood.

Detecting the client's words is helpful in building rapport, and will be evident when the following reactions are noticed in the client; note however, words account for only about 7% of communication, while 38% is based on voice tonality and 55% of rapport is reflected in physiology:

- Posture: angle of spine; head shoulder relationship; upper body position; lower body position
- Gestures
- Facial Expressions and Blinking
- Indicators of Rapport: feeling; color shift; client speaking/leading
- Breathing: rate and location

Analyzing Sensory Predicates helps build rapport, sensory awareness, outcome thinking and behavioral flexibility and helps to:

- Expand and use techniques beyond your own preferred way of communicating.
- "Get into their head"
- Understand strengths and weaknesses
- Help with learning (especially children)
- Increase awareness of the larger world perspective

SUBJECTIVE MODEL FAVORED IRS: Body Signals

It is also possible to interpret a client's IRS by interpreting body signals. To determine whether a client is visual, auditory, kinesthetic, etc., be on the lookout for helpful clues.

VISUAL

- Stands or sits upright with erect spine
- Eyes move up around the top
- High pitched, loud, fast speech

- Breathes at top of lungs
- Neat, tidy, well-groomed
- Not good at memorizing verbal instructions

KINESTHETIC

- Breathes from bottom of lungs
- Lower pitched, slower, quieter voice
- Moves slowly and deliberately
- Responds to touch and physical reward
- Stands closer than a visual person
- Memorizes by doing and walking through steps

AUDITORY DIGITAL

- Moves eyes from side-to-side
- Breathes from mid chest
- Talks to themselves
- Distracted by noises
- Repeats words back exactly
- Likes talking on phone
- Memorizes things by steps and sequences
- Sensitive to tone of voice

AUDITORY DIGITAL

- Talks to themselves
- Learns things by making sense of things
- Experiences tension in neck and shoulders

SUBJECTIVE MODEL FAVORED IRS: Eye-Accessing Cues

Finally, an intriguing way to interpret a client's Subjective Model IRS is to track eye movements.

LEFT SIDE: *Visually constructed images,* **Vc**, *Auditorily constructed sounds or words,* **Ac**, *and Kinesthetically constructed feelings* **K**.

RIGHT SIDE: *Visually remembered (eidetic) images,* **Vr**, *Auditorily remembered sounds,* **Ar**, *and Auditory words,* **A**. By watching the direction the eyes go when questioned, you can determine the client's preferred IRS.

Understanding a client's IRS is just one of thousands of useful NLP techniques and an integrative method of helping, persuading, and moving people where they want to be. It takes practice to perfect, but you will soon notice how easily you can gain rapport and interpret your client's perceptions of reality.

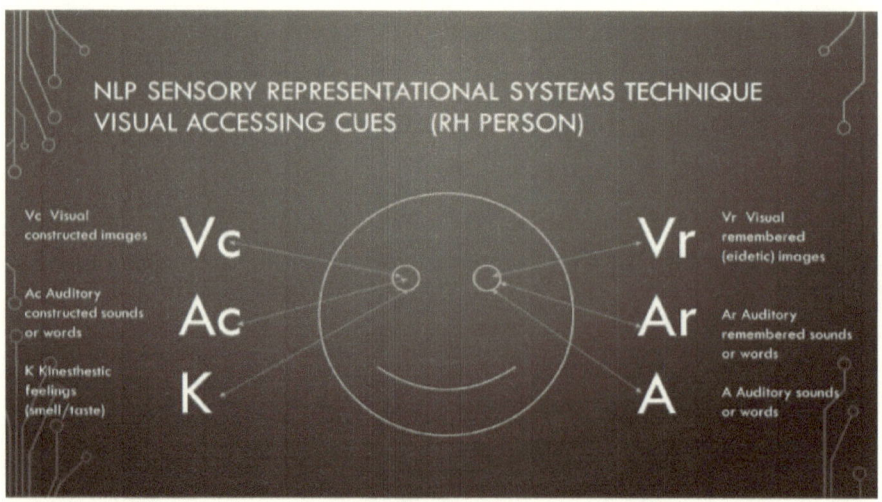

NLP SENSORY REPRESENTATIONAL SYSTEMS TECHNIQUE
VISUAL ACCESSING CUES   (RH PERSON)

Vc Visual constructed images — **Vc**

Ac Auditory constructed sounds or words — **Ac**

K Kinesthetic feelings (smell/taste) — **K**

Vr Visual remembered (eidetic) images — **Vr**

Ar Auditory remembered sounds or words — **Ar**

A Auditory sounds or words — **A**

IT'S TIME TO RECONSIDER HOW YOU USE AGE REGRESSION APPROACH IN HYPNOSIS

KELLEY T. WOODS

A HOT TOPIC in hypnosis forums is whether practitioners should or should not use RTC (Regress to Cause) approaches with their clients. For those who have been successfully helping clients with regression methodology for years, being challenged can feel not only like a professional, but a personal criticism. And for those who have never been taught RTC, it may be hard to understand why others may seem wedded or even dependent on it.

The concept of regression therapy involves a process wherein a therapist guides a client hypnotically to revisit earlier life memories, particularly events which are posited to have set a client's problem into play. Some clients consciously recall these experiences while others have no idea why they started having their problem. The belief of many RTC therapists is that unless these catalyzing memories are visited and addressed, the client's problem cannot be permanently resolved. Often, hypnosis is presented as the medium for doing this and clients are even promised that once the "cause" is discovered and dealt with, they will be spontaneously healed.

Austrian psychotherapist Sigmund Freud is credited with first coming up with regression therapy; he believed that traumatic memories are hidden in the subconscious. This approach has been used specifically for attempts to recover memories of sexual abuse, leading to a frenzy of unfortunate witch hunts in the late 1980s and 1990s. Researchers such as Elizabeth Loftus and Julia Shaw, among others, shed light on the myth of repressed memories. [1]

Current scientific research refutes the whole idea of repressed memory – there is no "hidden" depository of memories! [2] It's simply a metaphor, one that can be used effectively for our hypnosis clients, just like most of what we do. For hypnosis practitioners to continue to believe in these ideas does not best serve their clients and contains the risk of implanting false, unhelpful memories. Even a skilled and conscientious hypnotist can pollute the process with intonation, inflection or direct suggestion. [3]

One of the biggest problems in the use of regression techniques to discover what happened in a person's history lies with operator input – namely, the conscious or unconscious influence of the therapist. Many are familiar with the idea that the belief of the practitioner has influence on therapeutic outcome. A doctor's belief, for example, in the treatment they are prescribing can make a positive difference on its effectiveness for their patient. [4]

Hypnotists carry at least the same, if not more, weight when it comes to the approaches we use. It is believed that regression therapy works largely because people believe it works and because the human mind abhors ambiguity – we constantly try to put meaning to the things we experience in life. The idea that the answer to a problem we've struggled with may lie hidden in the subconscious appeals to many, especially when that is supported by a mind expert like a hypnotist!

Another problem with RTC lies within initial teaching of this regression model. I'll share my personal experience to demonstrate: In 2002, I finished my one-year hypnosis certification course at a local community college. Based largely on a client-centered model, my initial training included RTC as the primary approach for helping clients. I was taught to seek out and address SSEs (Subsequent Sensitizing Events), moving a client backwards on a timeline so that they could repeatedly revivify the events until they were de-sensitized or otherwise gained a different feeling. Eventually, we were instructed, we would end up at the original ISE (Initial Sensitizing Event) of the client's problem where the revivification and re-organizing would again be performed. This "discovery" process could require several and even many sessions, by the way.

As a person completely new to the field of hypnosis, and therapy in general, I found this all quite fascinating and accepted that RTC was an effective approach. Indeed, I falsely believed that because of the "magical" hypnotic state, there was no risk in using RTC. I understand that current instructors of such techniques may include warnings and caveats but, back in 2002, we were like kids being handed a chainsaw without any safety equipment!

Forward on a few years and I was building my private practice slowly, seeing clients on a part time basis. A doctor referred her patient to me – a woman who suffered intractable, unexplainable foot pain. Our first session together was amazing! I simply used one of the few pain-relieving tools I knew: progressive muscle relaxation. My client responded beautifully and found relief for the first time in years, so she booked a second session.

I thought long and hard about what I would do with this client in our next session. When she arrived, I had already decided that I would use RTC to permanently free her from this unnecessary pain! I was excited to play such an important role in this woman's life and began to use hypnosis to regress her to an earlier age when all of this unnecessary pain started. Within a short time, my client began to scream, grabbing at her foot. She blurted out, "My mother! My mother! We're in the car! She's dying!" Tears streamed down her face and she reached for her purse, avoiding my efforts to gain control of the situation. The last I saw of her was as she hurriedly exited my office and limped to her car.

My phone calls and emails went unanswered. I reached out to her doctor and let her know that our session had ended poorly. It took me quite a while to get my balance back, during which time I started to question the wisdom of what I had been taught. I recognized that I was limited in my skill set but I also wondered why a complete newbie would be given such a potentially volatile approach as their hypnosis mainstay.

Years later, I now understand that what my inept hypnotic bumbling triggered were the neural pathways related to the trauma of a 7 year-old child who had witnessed the death of her mother. My client had not informed me of her loss and I had no idea if she previously consciously remembered it or in what detail. Regardless, simply by asking her to imagine going to the source of her physical pain her brilliant mind, once relaxed, easily activated those associated memory nets. Because this occurred somewhat spontaneously, she had no safety net of mature perspective and was thrown into a panic state.

Today, I am immensely grateful for that poor client of mine and the painful lesson she taught because it ignited a career-long habit of questioning; not only things I am taught, but my own mindset. Is it necessary to throw the baby out with the bathwater? Of course not! I realize that there are no black and white answers when it comes to how we help our clients, but there are guidelines that can protect our clients while helping them.

Age regression remains an elegant hypnosis tool that can be used in many safe ways. One of the best applications is to elicit and anchor positive resource states – everyone has some experience of comfort, pleasure, confidence or success, so helping them isolate the memory (or imagined memory) and associated feelings creates a state that can utilized toward their goals.

Age regression is effective even without revivification; observing a version of a younger self from a dissociated perspective provides the opportunity for learning, reframing, self-acceptance, forgiveness, etc. When framed as a creative therapeutic process, an imaginative journey, the onus of dealing with painful or scary events is lessened or removed. Instead, a client can gain insight and even tap into what Dr. Herbert Benson coined as "Remembered Wellness". [5] What a wonderful use of the concept of the past!

If you are operating on a limiting paradigm of any kind in your hypnosis practice, you can free yourself and your clients by being flexible and expanding your knowledge. Learning from a variety of instructors and accessing a wide span of resources will help you find just the right approach that will safely fit any client.

References:

- [1] http://theconversation.com/explainer-what-are-false-memories-49454
- [2] https://blogs.scientificamerican.com/mind-guest-blog/memory-mondays-regression-therapy-isn-t-real-but-hollywood-keeps-the-myth-alive/ and http://bfms.org.uk/repression-a-theory-not-a-fact/
- [3] https://pdfs.semanticscholar.org/8323/da8765dd2f48de37d9bed6af7b5f9ace458e.pdf
- [4] https://www.ncbi.nlm.nih.gov/pmc/articles/PMC4518843/
- [5] https://www.pbs.org/bodyandsoul/218/benson.htm

COGNITIVE BEHAVIORAL HYPNOTHERAPY: THE LIMBIC SYSTEM

RICHARD D. DAMA, LPC

THIS IS part one of a two-part article outlining a practical theoretical framework called, Cognitive Behavioral Hypnotherapy (CBHt).

CBHt integrates Cognitive Behavioral Therapy with evidence-based aspects of NLP and Clinical Hypnotherapy. It is a solid, empirically validated framework for case conceptualization, (What is the client's real problem, where does it come from, and most importantly what is the payoff for this behavior?) and when combined with a firm understanding of the parts and processes of the Limbic System (LS), the appropriate treatment protocol becomes immediately apparent.

As hypnotherapists, our stock-in-trade is working with the subconscious mind but, does such a thing actually exist? If so, where is it? What does it really do and how does it work?

It will probably come as a surprise to many, but Neurophysiology has conclusively shown that the functions of the subconscious are tied to specific parts of the brain, each with highly specialized functions. This plexus of activity is called the Limbic System. In this, part one, we will discuss the parts, functions and effects of the limbic system and how they correlate to our work as therapists.

The advent of active brain scans now allows researchers to view the processes of the brain in real-time and have shown that human memory is holographic in nature. That is, rather than being stored in one discrete location in the brain, memory is a process in which several different lobes of the brain act together to house and process that memory. So too, there are different types of memory. Our short term and long-term memories are encoded and stored in different ways and in different parts of the brain. [1]

One of the clearest ways I have found to explain CBHt is to picture our brain as a computer. Like any computer, it needs programs to operate effectively. In real life, the programs are the things we learn, either academically or through experience. For example, one program enables us to tie our shoes; another allows us to drive a car, etc.

As with a computer, our brains need a master program or operating system that manages the hardware (our bodies) and all the other programs that the brain has at its disposal. In humans, this operating system is the subconscious mind in the form of the limbic system.

In general, therapists believe that the subconscious is where all experiences are stored as memory; where learning takes place; and where conscious thought originates.

So, let's turn our attention to the parts, care, and feeding of the Limbic System.

The Limbic System

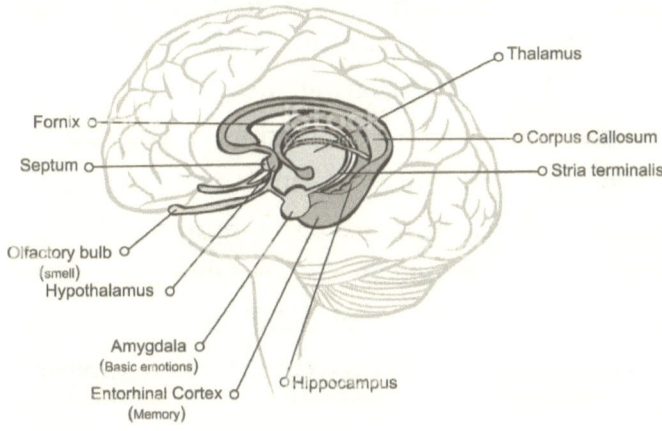

Amygdala:

This is the one area of the human brain that is probably responsible for the distress experienced by most of our clients, especially those with fear-based dysfunctional behaviors, such as anxiety, phobias, obsessive-compulsive disorder, etc.

Located in the temporal lobe, the amygdala; also called part of "Deep-brain"; is primarily responsible for integrating emotions with memories and the corresponding responses both psychologically and physically. In a very real sense, this is where our emotions and survival instincts meet. Together with the hippocampus, the amygdala generates an emotional lens through which all events and memories are filtered. Also, it is thought that due to its proximity to the prefrontal lobe it also can spur or inhibit our behavior, particularly anger and aggression.

In a groundbreaking 1999 study, Dr. Jim McGaugh and his team at the University of California at Irvine demonstrated that rats injected with norepinephrine and other Cortical Stress Hormones (CSH) just after having successfully traversed a maze, displayed significantly enhanced retention. Strong emotions lead to strong emotional memories. Think chronic PTSD with hypervigilance, fight/flight/freeze response to flashbacks, and your body constantly being flooded with adrenaline. [4]

On the other hand, Dr. Larry Cahill also at Irvine conducted a study in which subjects were given a CHS inhibitor and then asked to read an emotionally charged story and a similar emotionally neutral story. His results showed that subjects had a significantly lower rate of recall for the emotional story than they did for the neutral story. That implies that any emotionally charged situation that causes the release of CSH will produce stronger, more emotionally charged memories. In short, **emotionally charged situations biochemically lead to stronger memories**. [5]

Hypothalamus:

This lobe is located at the base of the brain, nestled below the Thalamus. The function of this body is to act as the primary regulator of the Autonomous Nervous System and has control over such actions as regulating body temperature, hormone secretion and maintaining physiological equilibrium.

For the therapist, it is vital to understand that this is the body that controls biologically programmed reactions such as fight or flight, reproduction, and feeding. Also vitally important is the fact that this lobe has no language. Instead, the currency of this body is pure instinct and emotion.

Mammillary Bodies (Not Shown):

These two structures lie on opposite sides of the midbrain One of the most important structures of the LS, they act as the primary relay nodes between the hippocampus, fornix, and thalamus. Moreover, "the role of the mammillary bodies in memory has been acknowledged since the late 1800s when mammillary body atrophy was observed in Korsakov's syndrome. Since then a number of findings---anatomical, clinical, and experimental---have supported and expanded upon a mnemonic role for the mammillary bodies". [3] It is also important to note that of the three main neural pathways, two of the three lead from the Hippocampus to the mammillary bodies and from the mammillary bodies to the thalamus with the flow of information exclusively in one direction. [4]

Hippocampus:

Continuing to follow the mind as a computer analogy, the Hippocampus is the registry of the memory. Located near the center of the brain, in the temporal lobe, this is one of the oldest parts of the brain. It is the body through which every event we have, are and will experience is filtered. In essence, this lobe receives cross-references and stores memory; especially those associated with strong emotions, spatial orientation, and long-term memory.

It is interesting to note, especially for clinical therapists that people who have suffered damage to the hippocampus are unable to make or retrieve short-term memories. With the number of traumatic brain injuries on the rise, this is a phenomenon we are sure to see more of in the future.

Cingulate Gyrus:

Main Sorter/Compiler for limbic system. The anterior cingulate gyrus is involved in the decision-making process. It does so by sensing deviations from desired outcomes. This function helps us in planning appropriate actions and responses, and with emotional bonding and attachment.

Working in tandem, the cingulate gyrus, and amygdala are responsible for forming conditioned fear responses and the memory association with sensory input from the thalamus. Collaboration between the cingulate gyrus and the hypothalamus control physiological responses such as when we experience emotions such as fear, anger, or excitement. These autonomic functions include heart rate, respiratory rate, and blood pressure regulation. Another important function of this body is spatial memory which involves the ability to perceive and process information regarding objects in the environment. [6]

Fornix:

The fornix: can be thought of like the fiber optic cable of the brain. It is the major output pathway from the hippocampus to the other parts of the limbic system.

So, What Does This Mean to Me?

By now, I sincerely hope you are beginning to see an open feedback loop between the various parts of the limbic system, the rest of the brain and body, and their role in forming memory in the form of biochemical impulses. These impulses are stored and accessed by specific lobes in the brain, each with a unique function and bio-mechanism. All of which act in concert with the body to produce behavioral responses to circumstances in the environment.

We as therapists become involved when the client's limbic system receives and accepts a program based on incomplete or incorrect information. An example, taken from my own practice involves an individual who came to me with a paralyzing fear of driving on main streets and absolutely refused to make left turns.

The client-related that they were driving to work on a snowy day. The streets were slippery and they were already feeling a sense of heightened alertness and respect for the conditions based on previous experience with slippery roads. This individual came to an intersection as the light turned green for them and they proceeded to make a left turn. During the turn, another driver was unable to stop in time and hit my client's car broadside (they were not injured...physically).

Using the preceding information regarding the limbic system, I explained to the client that their dysfunctional behaviors and negative emotions stemmed from a distortion the brain made between feelings of anxiety and fear and a safe outcome. I explained that because they were already in a state of heightened preparedness; I call it 'Pre-anxiety' for lack of a better term. When events began to rapidly escalate, the client understandably felt intense fear. The problem arose when the limbic system associated the fear with the successful outcome. Setting up a continuous loop of "if a little fear kept them safe that time, a lot of fear will keep them safer all the time".

With the help of hypnotherapy, the client was able to 'reprogram' the faulty behaviors through the process of Cognitive Behavioral Hypnotherapy. But that is a story for another edition.

I sincerely hope you will return for Part Two of CBHt Theory and Practice.

References

- [1] http://www.human-memory.net/intro_what.html
- [2] https://www.istockphoto.com/vector/cross-section-through-the-brain-showing-the-limbic-system-and-all-related-structures-gm873887584-244029307
- [3] Werf, Y. D., Witter, M. P., Uylings, H. B., Jolles, J. (2000). Neuropsychology of infarctions in the

thalamus: A review. Neuropsychologia, 38(5), 613-627.

- [4] Ferry, B., Roozendaal, B., McGaugh, J., (1999). Role of norepinephrine in mediating stress hormone regulation of long-term memory storage: a critical involvement of the amygdala. Biological Psychiatry, 46(9), 1140–1152.

- [5] Cahill, L., Prins, B., Weber, M., McGaugh, J. (1994). β-Adrenergic activation and memory for emotional events. Nature 371, 702–704.

www.SubliminalScience.com

FASTER TAPPING AS A USEFUL TECHNIQUE WITH CLIENTS

TONI MACRI REINER

YOU PROBABLY KNOW or have heard of some type of meridian tapping. There are many forms of Tapping and the general idea is that putting pressure on points along our meridian system will cause our thoughts, feelings and general emotional issues to begin to shift.

The modality of Tapping was originally taken from the ancient practice of acupuncture. Practitioners inserted fine needles into specific points along the meridians of the body to alleviate physical ailments. Today, Tapping is thought of as "emotional acupuncture."

A chiropractor in the 1960's, George Goodheart Jr., explored the connection between the meridians and their association with certain body parts and illnesses. In 1964, he advanced his earlier research by developing a method of muscle testing known as Applied Kinesiology. [1] During this time, he became aware that the emotional state of the patient affected the response and strength of the muscles being tested.

A psychiatrist named John Diamond, one of Dr. Goodhart's students, simplified the process of associating certain body parts and illnesses. Through trial and error, he found which emotion(s) corresponded to each meridian.

Roger Callahan, another student of Dr. Goodhart's group, began to combine the responses of the meridians. This led to the creation of the "Karate Chop," which is the Tapping area on the outside of the palm. This meridian correlated to the small intestine. Callahan also found that merging certain meridian points correlated with specific emotional issues and that reciting affirmations while addressing these areas increased the effectiveness of the tapping. He became known for TFT (Thought Field Therapy) which consists of Tapping on points while holding the problem in one's mind.

Gary Craig who created EFT (Emotional Freedom Technique) and Patricia Carrington (Accutap) are also pioneers who developed their own systems of Tapping. Other meridian techniques that have grown from the earlier discoveries include: "Be Set Free Fast" (BSFF), "Tapas Acupressure Technique" (TAT), "Simplified Energy Therapy" (SET), "Provocative Energy Therapy" (PET), and "Eutaptics" (FEFT). You may hear the term Meridian Tapping Techniques (MTT) used by practitioners as a general term.

The methodology of all these variations is putting pressure (Tapping, rubbing or touching) on an acupuncture point associated with a certain organ will change or dissipate the problem or diminish its importance. The techniques can be used for many issues ranging from anxiety, fear, cravings, etc.

As with many techniques, practitioners like to tweak and adjust them in order to develop the best way to enhance the effectiveness for their clients.

The style that works best is up to each practitioner based on what resonates with the specific client at the time. I personally use FEFT (Faster EFT/Eutaptics) from Robert Smith.[2] Tapping is my go-to for beginning the majority of all my sessions. It is a quick and easy way to teach a client how to "scratch and alter" the recorded history of a problem. The other reason I use it first, especially with smokers, is that it instills confidence in a client that they can change. At the end of a round of Tapping, they have set up a positive anchor or "Good Place" which they can immediately return to.

Asking great questions in the very beginning of the session allows the practitioner to find out what resources the clients bring with them. What do they want to achieve by working with you?

Listening closely for their metaphoric language allows you to speak in terms the client understands. Their language is what I want to use when teaching them or using Tapping. I do NOT guess what's going on, I always use their own concept of their issue.

Most of the time our clients want to tell us "the story" around their issue(s). "This happened, that happened, she did this, he does that, etc." All we really need to know is "how they know" they have a problem. Life happens, and when a problem occurs, "How Do You Know" it's a problem for you?

To know you have a problem you may say, "I feel anxious or I see red." How do you specifically "Do" anxiety? Are you thinking, seeing a memory, or hearing the tone of voice? Many smokers say "they just know" it is time to smoke. Helping a client get in touch with the way their body responds to a feeling can be the first step in teaching them to be mindful. Once assessed, Tapping, touching or rubbing the points begins. There is no set up statement or karate chop point used in the style I prefer. There are several important steps used when Tapping. (I like to keep it simple so the client will use it.) Once "how they know" is assessed the Tapping starts. I guide them where to tap.

As they tap, they will **ONLY focus** on the feeling of their fingers. This focus moves neurons away from the problem state and the Tapping disrupts the pattern. As I previously mentioned, words used while Tapping are specific words or phrases they have expressed to describe their issue.

The client focuses on "How They Know" and then I ask them to notice the sensation of their fingers while Tapping on each of the meridian points. After Tapping 5-6 times on each of 4 the points, we end by grasping the wrist, taking a deep breath, exhaling it out and go to their good place or happy memory. (This anchored safe place has been set up beforehand.)

The neurons fire from the problem area to a good place causing the problem area to loosen and it begins dissolving. There are many changes occurring in the mind and body while Tapping. It's important to keep the procedure simple so the client can understand the change process.

Cravings, anxiety, stress, fears and many other issues can be addressed with Tapping. Anytime a client is already associated into a problem, disrupting it quickly while moving them into a positively anchored state shows them just how fast they can change. Some clients move very quickly through an issue and sometimes even past larger obstacles. For others the process may be slower.

Using the SUDS (Subjective Units of Distress Scale: 0-10) after a session, I've had a serious drinker go from the thought/fear (rated 10) "When can I drink again?" to a 1, not being able to find the thought at all.

Smokers are great clients for this technique. They come in wanting a cigarette, we rate it with the SUDS, then tap on the "How They Know" they want to smoke. The craving goes down. It not only shows them they can eliminate or at least manage the initial cravings but gives them hope. It truly makes believers out of them. I always tell them it might seem like a weird thing to do, but it works!

When I teach this technique to children, I frame it as "Did you know you have magic in your fingertips?" When I explain how they can be in control of themselves and decide how they WANT to feel, I usually have a quick buy-in.

Fears are another issue where Tapping can really help loosen the grip of fear. I've recently worked with a number of cheerleaders and gymnasts. Quite often they've injured themselves by falling or just feel blocked in a certain place in their routine.

Teaching them Tapping can move the worry or fear away and make it seem less important. It is empowering to teach our clients how to help themselves. After all, no one gives you a handbook at birth to teach you how to manage the emotions you feel while on your journey!

Tapping is a fantastic tool!

References:

- [1] Thrivingnow.com/Historyoftapping
- [2] Robert Smith FEFT

IDEAS ON CREATING POWERFUL DIRECT SUGGESTIONS BASED ON THE HIERARCHY OF VALUES (HIERARCHY OF CRITERIA)

LEONARDO SILVÉRIO

WHAT IS MORE important for you, to feel INTENSITY in your life or to know that you are being RESPONSIBLE? This question may sound weird but, a long time ago, I was asked this same question. Without hesitation, I answered that both denoted Values which were very important for me but that, to some extent, I would sacrifice the idea of being responsible in the exchange of more intensity in my life. So, in general, Intensity > Responsible. For me.

And this was not the only question I had to answer. In fact, I was asked to classify, in order of importance, a list of values like Family, Success, Respect, Justice and more, all of them very important for me. At the end of the exercise, I was left with a list called "Hierarchy of Core Values". It was like:

Order of Priority	VALUE
1	*Family*
2	*Professional Success*
3	*Intensity*
4	*Responsibility*
5	*Respect*
6	*Justice*
etc.	etc.

If you have already learned NLP or Coaching, you may have done this same exercise at some point in your learning path. You may even do it today with your clients or, perhaps, members of your team. What I want here is to anlyse how hipnotic this process of obtaining the prioritized list of Values is and, also, discuss some ideas about how you can use it to write effective Direct or Indirect Suggestions, to the benefit of your client.

One thing that you may have already noticed is that, when people manage to relate the Hyerarchy of Criteria with current behaviorial complaints, they will change their state radically. I still remember how "magical" I felt in the moment when I understood why I was procrastinating: as Intensity was, for me, more important than Responsibility, I would leave most tasks to "the last minute". This (self-imposed) time pressure would make me feel very intense and then, in this state, I would do the job in the best way I could. Following this strategy, I would do what I had to do -

being responsible - and intense at the same time. Nice but, of course, I was always risking not doing the task very well, which was not nice at all. With this new understanding of my procrastination, everything made sense to me. I also remember that I, literally, started day-dreaming when I had this insight.

As, described above, many times you will notice that this exercise is so insightful that people fall automatically into a hypnotic trance, sometimes a light one, other times very deeply, with their eyes opened. This "moment of enlightenment" works just as a pattern interruption induction because it is, indeed, a pattern interruption. You will also notice that your authority (as a specialist) increases. So, natural trances plus authority... what more could a hypnotist ask for?

If you want to know more about the Hierarchy of Criteria, you can learn this process in books like K. Burton (2011) or searching "hierarchy+criteria+nlp" in the Internet. If you allow me a hint, it is important, when using this process, to never judge the person's Values or it's priority Order. Remember, the map is not the territory!

What I want to explore with you now is: "how can we use this process to create more powerful direct or indirect suggestions?" You know already that the Hierarchy of Criteria provides you with authority and promotes natural trance states... but there is much more in it! It gives you important data about how the person motivates him/herself: Values which are higher positioned in the list will be more motivational and, with this knowledge, you can now make your suggestion more desirable to be followed. Also, the person will trust that he/she is able to act upon the suggestion because, now, there is a new and much more precise level of understanding of the problem they wanted to solve.

Direct Suggestion Formula

When creating Direct Suggestions, I like to follow the ideas proposed by R. Nongard (2011). An effective Direct Suggestion has the following segments: the new behaviour, plus the reason why it is going to work, plus motivation. The "reason why" segment can be just a phrase like "and this will happen naturally because, now, your unconscious mind knows much better". The "motivation" segment can be any link connecting the new behaviour to the higher values in the list. So, a basic "formula" of an effective suggestion is:

"From this point forward, you no longer do **W**... but instead you **X**... and you will find it easy to do because of **Y**... and this new behaviour will result in **Z**."

Let's analyze this formula and understand why it works so well: first, you remember the person about the behaviour he/she doesn't want to do again (**W**) and, doing so, the person will recall what triggers the problem. You then give the suggestion of what to do (**X**) instead, which is the new strategy you want the person to follow. At this point, there may be an attempt to doubt the suggestion: imagine the person thinking "oh, I don't think that I will be able to do **X** because it seems so hard". That's when you say **Y**, explaining why they are ready to do it, kind of shutting up their internal dialog. And, finally, remember them of the "final prize", that is, motivate them to follow your suggestion! For this, use the Hierarchy of Values: the higher the Value is in the list, the more motivated he/she will be to act.

Example

Considering the example I have already mentioned - "procrastination" - a powerful suggestion could be:

> "From this point forward, you no longer leave everything to the last minute… but instead, you feel a desire to do things right away… a desire which will come to you naturally just because, now, your unconscious mind understands things much better… doesn't it? That's right… and I wonder if you have already considered how this new behaviour will inspire people in your family, specially the younger ones."

Or:

> "From this point forward, you no longer leave things to the last minute… but, instead, you do them as soon as possible… as this will make you feel even more intense, and intensity is something that your mind naturally seeks, right? And I am curious to know if finishing the tasks earlier will now allow you to be more relaxed, having more quality time with your family."

Both above examples were created using the Hierarchy. You will find out that having the Hierarchy and the Direct Suggestion formula, you are now able to deliver suggestions which are powerful, effective and very tailored to he person you are helping.

I hope you find this idea useful!

References

- Kate Burton, "Coaching With NLP for Dummies", 2011, chapter 8, Wiley Publishing
- Richard K Nongard, "Magic Words in Hypnosis", 2011, page 60, PeachTree Professional Education, Inc.

DECREASING ANTICIPATORY RESPONSE OF NAUSEA IN CHEMOTHERAPY

JAMES MALONE

NAUSEA IS a common and unpleasant side effect of chemotherapy in cancer treatment and it also occurs in many women during pregnancy, especially in the first trimester. With these situations, there is most definitely a biochemical reason why the nausea occurs. Vomiting is one way the body protects itself by releasing what it perceives as toxic or foreign. However, due to the way the brain learns through making associations, the symptom can also be triggered by other stimuli. For example, sight or scent of food once enjoyed by that individual can bring about an attack. Indeed, anticipatory thoughts alone can bring about queasiness. It's as if the person is unconsciously trained to become sick in certain situations.

I have heard of many professional hypnotists in the past who have used their skills to help those with anticipatory nausea, and in this article I will share how I expanded upon this. Last year, I had a former client reach out for help with the anticipatory nausea she was experiencing related to chemotherapy for breast cancer. While preparing for the session, I stumbled across an article where it had been found that sniffing isopropyl alcohol, the kind used in prep pads prior to injection, can stave off nausea. The article mentions a study in the "Annals of Emergency Medicine" where sniffing alcohol actually outperformed the leading prescription medicine for nausea.

Although the physical mechanism as to why this works apparently is not clear, it has been proven to be effective nonetheless, so an idea struck me. During the preliminary talk, I told the client about this study and showed her a copy of the article as a form of 'social proof'. (You can find a copy of the article I used by searching for "A Cure for Nausea: Try Sniffing Alcohol" by Nicholas Bakalar from the 3/13/18 edition of the New York Times. You might want to save a copy you can print out as needed for your clients.)

I then asked if it would be alright during the hypnosis session if I wiped the back of her hand with a prep pad and then asked her to sniff it a few times, to which she agreed. It is a wise idea to always ask for prior permission if any type of physical contact is going to take place during a session. After induction and deepener, I said something to the effect of, "In a moment I am going to wipe the back of your hand with the prep pad like I mentioned before. When you notice a cooling sensation, please lightly nod yes and relax even more deeply." Due to the way alcohol evaporates quickly it is almost impossible not to feel a cooling sensation, so it creates a vivid real time sensory experience. This is in some ways like the famed 'magnetic fingers' suggestibility experiment where a natural physiological response, the natural contraction of the finger muscles, takes care of the effect.

After she nodded in the affirmative that she felt the cooling sensation, I held the pad under her nose and asked to take a few deep sniffs and then suggested, "anytime you take a whiff of a prep pad like that you are going to notice a pleasant cooling and calming sensation just like the one you now have on the back of your hand traveling down your esophagus, into the stomach and the rest of your digestive tract, as well as the centers of the brain that keep the digestive tract moving in the right direction." I compounded with other kinds of suggestions and pleasant somatic images of a future where eating is gradually becoming more pleasurable, energy levels increase and other personally relevant details.

Afterward I gave her some prep pads and a printout of the article. Upon follow up she reported feeling much better and actually didn't need to sniff the pad. Similar results were experienced with another cancer patient and a woman with severe morning sickness around the same time period. What's kind of cool is that this combines a safe, inexpensive and effective over the counter remedy that few people have heard about along with the power of suggestion. The prep pad becomes a tool the client can carry with her wherever she goes. Being enable to decrease anticipatory nausea can have a profound effect on a person's quality of life. In the case of cancer care, some patients have been known to discontinue potentially life-saving treatments due to the unpleasant side effects. Many women afflicted with morning sickness find otherwise wanted pregnancies too much to bear. The potential for the professional hypnotist to make a positive difference in these situations is great.

References

- 3/4/2019 nausea article - Google Docs - https://docs.google.com/document/d/1Xa0dxZe_QuerqLn_xjMgSffn18WeS7q ECBBiWohowzY

PATHWAY TO TRUE HEALING: HOW TO HEAL CELLULAR MEMORIES

PATRICIA ESLAVA VESSEY, PCC, CHT.

HAVE you ever heard an old song from your high-school days and suddenly felt emotional; maybe happy, sad or nostalgic? Maybe you can even remember tastes or smells associated with those memories. How do you feel when you think about seeing your best friend or beloved pet? Chances are you feel those good feelings somewhere in your body.

Other emotions are stored in your body, as well. For example, stressful feelings may manifest as tension in the jaw, shoulders or stomach. The fear of public speaking can be felt in the body as trembling, shortness of breath and anxiety. Conversely, sensations in the body like pain, pressure, tightness or even injury are most often related to an emotion being felt.

Each person has a carefully crafted and powerful mind-body relationship. Every experience and emotion is memorialized and stored in the physical and the mental body. At will, people can recall names, faces, places, feelings and sometimes even scents and scenarios from long ago. Though some may forget many of these memories over time, they're permanently etched in cellular memories, leaving physiological imprints.

How and where are memories stored?

For a long time, scientists believed that memories were formed, processed, and sent to different destinations in the brain. *Dr. Wilder Penfield*, an American-Canadian neurosurgeon, was one of the first to accidentally discover this. In the 1950s while working on an epilepsy cure, he electrically stimulated different areas of his patients' brains while they were under local anesthesia. He discovered that when he stimulated various regions, they produced specific memories in the patient's life. This discovery led to the long-held belief that we store memories in the brain; however, in 2004 there was a huge medical breakthrough in this area. During a research study at Southwestern University Medical Center in Dallas, scientists discovered that memories are stored in the tissues, organs, and cells of the body, not just the brain.

The late *Candace Pert*, a neuropharmacologist and author of *Molecules of Emotion*, National Institutes of Health (NIH) Georgetown University Medical Center, made several ground-breaking discoveries and contributions in the area of cellular memories. Her research started a revolution in beliefs and a theory about how our thoughts and emotions are capable of creating wellness or disease in our bodies.

Dr. Pert and many other scientists believe that our emotional memories including all injuries and traumas are stored in multiple locations in the tissues of the body, "not just, or even primarily, in the brain." These thoughts and emotions "bubble up" from the body which are processed and give meaning to life according to individual beliefs. She believed that the body is the subconscious mind and that people can't heal solely by talking about their memories. Dr. Pert states, however, *"We can access our mind and our emotions through the physical body. We need to get in touch with our body through some mind-body work to access, heal, and release stuck emotions and traumas."*

Organ Transplants and Cellular Memories

According to cellular memory theory, memories and even personality traits, are not only stored in the brain but are also stored in the various organs in the body, such as the heart, lungs and liver. The best way to understand cellular memory is by reviewing organ transplant stories.

There are many extraordinary stories about transplant recipients acquiring traits from their donors. One famous and fascinating story is about Claire Sylvia, a health-conscious professional dancer, choreographer, and recipient of a heart and lung transplant. After her transplant, she began acting differently and having strange dreams which later turned out to be about her donor. She developed a craving for beer, burgers and chicken nuggets, which she didn't eat before. Claire also started wearing different colors and liking different music. Later, she discovered that these preferences were those of her 18-year-old donor. These experiences so impacted her that she wrote about them in her book, *A Change of Heart*. These and many other transplant cases demonstrate that cellular memories are not only permanently stored in the organs and tissues, but they can also be transferred to the recipients and even change their personality.

Healing Cellular Memories

This cellular memory theory applies to all without exception. Cells are imprinted with history of every experience up to the present, and, these experiences dictate thoughts, beliefs, feelings, and behavior. A history of unhealed stress, drama, trauma, and anger, may cause the same emotions to continue to resurface. The brain uses cellular memories to determine how to respond to everything in life. This is why the same unhealthy and unsafe choices may keep being made, even though consciously a person may know better.

According to scholars, there's no true healing without healing the cellular memories - physically or non-physically! Willpower, traditional therapy, and even conscious desensitization are not very effective because they don't get to the source of the real problem. Nor do these methods provide lasting cellular healing. Instead, often they program your unconscious to repress those memories and disconnect your emotional responses from them. This is merely coping, not cellular healing, often causing people to feel numb, stressed and unable to cope effectively. Traditional therapy can go on for years and fail to bring about true healing growth and change.

For true healing, the source must be located and healed. The source, is the original cellular memory that's triggering the reaction. Doing this will change the response that is negatively impacting your body.

Treatment Modalities

Scientist Howard Hall proved that the cellular function in the immune system can be trained using modalities such as self-hypnosis, biofeedback, guided imagery, relaxation, and autogenic training. These interventions can help actively influence our health and healing. Individuals can work to retrain, rewire, and heal memories in the immune system and throughout the body.

The conventional therapeutic techniques for emotional regulation and healing work concentrate mostly on cognitive strategies. However, one of the most readily available but underused strategies for change work and healing is *using body movement. Antonio Damasio,* a neuroscientist, states that emotions are generated in the body and sent to the brain. This concept implies that through deliberate control of motor behavior (movement), you can adjust your emotions and affect your feelings, thoughts and actions.

Thoughts and emotions manifest through the body in words and movement. Through movement, the unconscious mind notices information or cues that the conscious mind hardly sees. The body is also a great source of self-knowledge and wisdom, and because cellular memories are stored in the various tissues of the body, movement-based therapies like HypnoKinesthetics (that uses hypnosis,) coaching, NLP and movement in healing work, the emotional effects of those memories can heal and change.

Everything that has happened to in life has been downloaded into the tissues and organs in the body. These cellular memories influence all aspects of thoughts, feelings, and behavior. If left unhealed and unresolved, these cellular memories can lead to unhappiness, ill health, failure, and devastation.

Historic events cannot be changed, but the memories of trauma, abuse, neglect, disappointment, unhappiness, and failure, stored in the body can be healed and changed. With alternative treatment modalities like hypnosis, Neuro-Linguistic Programming (NLP)biofeedback, autogenic training, HypnoKinesthetics, and others, one can access, heal, release and replace the unhelpful cellular memories with new empowering ones.

References

- Penfield, Dr. Wilder. *Cellular Memories* http://sites.bu.edu/ombs/2014/11/11/is-the-brain-the-only-place-that-stores-our-memories/
- *Medical Breakthrough*, 2004. https://www.consciouslifestylemag.com/cellular-memory-healing-clearing/
- Pert, Candace. *The Research of Candace Pert, Ph.D.* https://www.equilibrium-e3.com/images/PDF/The%20Research%20of%20Candace%20Pert.pdf
- Claire, Sylvia. *A Change of Heart: Memoir.* My Book
- Hall, Howard. https://www.equilibriume3.com/

images/PDF/The%20Research%20of%20Candace%20Pert.pdf

- Damasio, Antonio.: https://www.ncbi.nlm.nih.gov/pmc/articles/PMC5033979/
- Damasio, A.: https://www.technologyreview.com/s/528151/the-importance-of-feelings/
- Damasio, A.: http://www.loc.gov/loc/brain/emotion/Damasio.html

BEDWETTING AND THE HYPNOTIST

SETH-DEBORAH ROTH, RN, CRNA, CCHT

ONE OF THE most distressing calls a hypnotist gets is from a mother who is at her wits end—her child is still wetting the bed. They have tried everything: bedwetting alarms that ring after the bed is soaked, waterproof rubber sheets, pills that dry up the child like a prune, yet they still wake up soaked in urine. So before we talk about how we as hypnotists can help, let's learn a little bit about how the bladder works.

The bladder is a muscular organ that can hold up to two cups of urine. Circular muscles, called sphincters, help keep urine from leaking. The sphincters close tightly like a rubber band around the opening of the bladder into the urethra. Nerves in the bladder tell you when to urinate. The sensation becomes stronger until the bladder reaches its limit. The nerves send a message to the brain and the urge to empty your bladder intensifies. The brain signals the bladder muscles to tighten, squeezing urine out of the bladder. At the same time, the brain signals the sphincter muscles to relax and then the urine leaves the bladder.

Bedwetting is a heartbreaking problem for both child and family. It is especially hard for the child who is experiencing the problem. It impacts the child at a very deep level at a time when the concept of "self" is developing. Imagine not being able to go to sleepovers with your friends because you still have to wear "big boy" or "big girl" diapers when you are thirteen. Or imagine not going to sleepover camp because you wake up in a puddle of urine every night. No overnight school trips or soccer tournament trips either. It's a secret nobody knows other than your mom or your dad. Sometimes mom and dad won't even talk about the problem because they don't want to hurt your feelings, yet the issue is always there. Imagine the unspoken frustration of your mother who gets up to change the bed (sometimes the frustration is even visible because she is so tired). Or the sad face of your dad even though he is "trying" to hide it.

There are two components that the hypnotherapist needs to work with: the physical and the emotional. When working with the physical, remember that when we are speaking to the subconscious, we are giving instructions to the physical. Repetition is key to developing a new neural pathway and taking advantage of brain plasticity. Possible suggestions vary with the imagination.

Here are some suggestions:

- Use the idea of locking up the bladder with a large, strong key and a sentry that stands guard and sends a signal from the bladder to the brain.
- Use the visualization of taking an imaginary visit to the bladder muscle and practice holding tight then letting the urine out in the morning.
- Talk about how the body knows how to stay dry

during the day and is learning how to stay dry at night and the brain is learning how to make the special potion to help them stay dry at night.

- If your bladder gets full, the feeling of pressure is so strong when the bladder gets full that you cannot continue to sleep you must get up.
- Use ideas in the phrasing which allows for the learning: "I wonder how you'll feel when you wake up in the morning and you realize you bed is dry. It may be tomorrow morning, or the next morning or the morning a little while from now. But, one morning you will wake up and realize that you are growing up and your bed is dry and you have been dry all night."

Metaphors are also a wonderful tool to use with children. Perhaps it is the idea of a whale with its blow hole opening and closing and staying closed while under water, or perhaps one is telling a story of learning and changing and growing up. Sometimes there are emotional issues that must be dealt with.

I remember working with an eleven-year-old boy for bedwetting. His parents were divorced and he was living with his mom. His bedwetting resolved and then returned after his visits to his dads house. Obviously, there were some emotional issues that needed to be addressed. Usually, you find yourself needing to install some confidence into the bedwetting child who has been made fun of for years or feels inadequate or feels like a failure.

I would like to end this article by sharing a testimonial I received from the parents of a boy I worked with. When you read this you will understand the impact we can have on our clients as well as their family. I don't know about you, but for me, there is no better feeling in the world than to know I have helped to influence someone's life for the better.

"Imagine having dinner with your child who has enuresis and he pours himself a huge glass of milk and you don't think twice about it. We have worked for five years to help him be dry with no success. Our son was dry five out of seven nights from the first week of treatment and the success only increased to being totally dry after three sessions. We are so very grateful and so glad to see our son so proud of himself."

— THRILLED PARENTS

FREE WEIGHT LOSS HYPNOSIS SCRIPT: FOUR SESSIONS TO A NEW LIFE

HYPNOSIS SESSION !:

Adding new things to life

Pre-talk

People often ask if hypnosis is really helpful in losing weight and restoring physical health. If you have never experienced hypnosis yourself, perhaps you are skeptical of such a claim. Hypnosis isn't a magic bullet, of course. You won't open your eyes after a session to find yourself one hundred pounds lighter. Hypnosis is not about magic, but about learning. In this session, you will learn new things, and as a result take new actions. In fact, this session is not about giving up anything. You do not have to give up old patterns after this session. Rather, it is about adding new things to life.

After years of doing addiction counseling, I have discovered that people often have a fear about giving something up or about their abilities to do so. I have also found that people often really don't want to give up some of the old patterns of life. The reason for this is that even though they may be unhealthy, the old pattern serves some purpose.

What works is not giving something up, but gaining something. Therefore, the purpose of this session is threefold. First, it will teach you how to enter a state of hypnosis. Second, it will teach new habits for you to incorporate as a part of your new lifestyle. Finally, it will give you hope. Even though you may have tried and failed in the past, these sessions are not about trying to reach a magic number. Rather, they will help your body naturally become the ideal weight that you should be. Each individual is different and you intuitively know what your needs are. By focusing on adding new things to life rather than trying to take away old things, you will have a newfound ability to effortlessly accomplish what is most important to you.

Why is it important to learn how to enter a state of hypnosis? Hypnosis is a natural state, not a mystical one. We actually enter hypnosis each day without even thinking about it. Hypnosis is not like the things we see in Hollywood. You will not be a mindless drone. Nor will you mindlessly follow absurd commands. Rather, you will be able to use hypnosis to improve learning and to embed new lessons into your subconscious mind. Have you ever said to yourself, "I am going to lose weight"? Yet, a few weeks later you realized that you made that decision but still weighed the same, or even more? This is because you made a decision with the conscious mind, the part that is temporal and acts in the moment, rather than the subconscious mind.

In hypnosis, we are exactly the opposite of what Hollywood portrays. Like in meditation, we are more focused, goal-directed, and intuitively aware. Like an old-time cassette tape, you can record over the messages and the negative behavioral patterns of the past. This is why we will not be giving up anything in this first session. As you add new patterns and new lessons to your life, you will naturally and intuitively replace old patterns.

There are several new habits that you will add to your life in this first session. First, you will add food to your diet. You will add nutrient rich foods that are the source of natural energy and health. If you do this each day for a week, you will find that you will effortlessly eat less of the unhealthy things that may have been a part of your life. You will also add a new method of eating. The result will be recording over old patterns that, in the past, have been destructive. You will also add new activities to life and increase your daily physical activity. Most importantly, you will begin a wonderful journey that will transform into a new chapter of life.

The first step is to learn how to enter a state of hypnosis. For beginners, the easiest way to do this is to use guided relaxation. In fact, because guided relaxation is a great way to manage stress, it will be your first new skill for managing weight. Many of our unhealthy patterns come from emotional reactions to stress. Most people never take the time, like you are doing today, to learn how to practice this skill.

So, by going though this basic process you will have already added a tool that can be useful to you. Relaxation is a way of entering hypnosis because in a relaxed state we are open to new lessons and are comfortable considering new options. There is no right or wrong way to experience this. Begin by getting comfortable in your chair. In a few minutes, you will be very relaxed. However, you will always be attentive, able to hear my voice, and aware of your surroundings. You might hear outside noises, but these will not distress you. In fact, they will reassure you that you are exactly where you need to be, doing exactly what you need to be doing.

Now that you have found a comfortable place to still the body and the mind, begin by scanning your body. Anywhere you are carrying the tension of the day in your muscles, simply let those muscles relax. Pay attention to the small muscles of the brow and around the eyes. Let them relax as well. Often, tension is held in muscles of the jaw. You can even allow these muscles to relax.

As you relax, notice that your breathing becomes slower and more natural. As you listen to the quiet in the room or hear the distant sounds of others outside of the room, give yourself permission to enjoy this time of developing a sense of deep relaxation.

As your hands rest on your lap, let them feel very relaxed, very heavy, and very calm. Again, scan your body and relinquish any remaining tension. Relax any remaining tension held in the shoulders, back, or legs. Now, notice that your breathing is slower and calm. In just a few moments, your heart rate has even slowed.

This basic process of physical relaxation can also be used to still the mind. Do not worry if your mind has been wandering or thinking. After all, this is what minds do. Imagine yourself under a clear blue sky. You can imagine that you are in a place you have been to before, would like to go, or a place entirely of your own creation. In the sky, there is a single white puffy cloud, gently drifting towards the horizon. As it drifts, send all of your thoughts, cares, and concerns into that cloud. Watch the cloud move farther and farther towards the horizon, until it disappears all together. Now, both your body and mind are completely relaxed. If any other thoughts surface, just allow them to drift towards the horizon after that puffy cloud.

In this state of hypnosis, I am going to give you some direct suggestions. These are not suggestions that come from me, rather they are suggestions you have asked me to make by participating in this session. I am also going to share what are called indirect suggestions to help you to learn intuitively. I know you have a strong sense of what is good for you, because people who participate in these types of sessions usually do. As a result, learning intuitively will be easy for both your conscious and subconscious mind. The direct suggestions I am going to make will add to your life. I will also share with you some of my own personal experiences, for the path you are on is well-worn.

It is amazing how easy it is for someone to lose weight by adding something into their life, even by adding more food. By adding nutrient dense foods into your diet, your body will naturally and effortlessly respond in ways that are best for it. So by adding something into your life each day, you will be well on your way to a slimmer, lighter, and healthier you.

The first addition will be adding one pound of fruit and one pound of vegetables to your diet each day. It is amazing how by cutting up a bowl of fruit and a bowl of vegetables, one begins to crave health. Many who have done this have had that very experience. By adding a pound of fruit and a pound of vegetables into your diet each day, you will be just like the others who have made this beneficial change to their lives.

I grew up in Chicago and I remember, as a child, driving with my grandmother to Great Lakes Navel training station. While we were there, we would go to the PX to do our grocery shopping. Each week, on what I assume was my grandfather's payday, we would shop for groceries. My grandmother would cut coupons for our weekly shopping ritual. I remember how long it took to shop and how many bags my grandmother would buy. When we got home, I would help her put the groceries away. We stored some in the kitchen and some in the deep freezer in our garage. I spent the rest of my adult life shopping the way I learned to shop with my grandmother, by making a weekly visit to the store and coming home with a week's supply of groceries.

In 2004, I spent a great deal of time overseas. I had an opportunity to travel to Eastern Europe and to Asia, where I spent my time with local families rather than simply exploring as a tourist. In almost every place I visited on three different continents, the people shopped the same way for food. In every home I stayed in, the families went shopping each day for a small amount of groceries. While walking home in the afternoons, we shopped for dinner. We always selected fresh foods, fruits, and vegetables. We usually only purchased the quantity that we would need for that night. It seemed like we were always in the express lane, choosing a few items in a basket and checking out quickly, rather than shopping for a hundred items to last a week.

And, I noticed a difference. When I began shopping each day, the food was fresh and there was no need to purchase frozen prepared foods, which are usually processed and unhealthy. And so, I began to shop in this new way even upon my return to America. Each day, I stop at the market by my house, usually buying fruit for the next day and a few items for dinner that night. You will also find great benefit in adding a trip to the supermarket in your daily routine and choosing a limited amount of food on each trip. Simply, purchase enough to last for the next day or two.

Transitional Deepener

Confusion

It may seem odd to lose weight by gaining so many things. This, of course, is the paradox of life. It really doesn't matter if you look at a clock and see that is it lunchtime, dinnertime, or even time for a snack. By adding healthy foods such as fruits and vegetables, any time is the right time for you. It is the right time to be confident in your additions to life, the right time to lose weight by gaining new habits, and the right time to enjoy being you.

Double Bind

During this week, you will not weigh yourself on a scale. The numbers are no longer important. Adding new experiences to life is what is important. Your body is intuitive and will either lose weight quickly or slowly, but healthy additions to life always result in change. Of course, the results of this addition will be achieving your goal of decreasing your weight and increasing your health.

I am going to take a moment to give you some direct suggestions. The suggestions do not come from me. Rather, they are things you have asked me to suggest by participating in this session. Immediately and without hesitation, you will take action on each of these suggestions, being reminded each day to act on them. How will you remember? It is easy.

Before we go any further, let yourself feel the emotions of

success that you desire. Take a moment to visualize yourself as you know you will be, six months from now, a year from now, and even a few years from now. See yourself healthy and vibrant. You can even listen to the new "you" telling you how wonderful it feels to have shed so many old patterns. Feel the energy and emotion of success from the "you" that you would like to be.

Right here and now, let those future progressions exist inside of you. You see, anything we can create with our mind is already in existence within us. All of the wonderful feelings of success and the sight of the new you is already present, deep within you. It really isn't hard to move towards health because we are not really creating or reinventing a new you. Rather, we are drawing the real you to the surface. Enjoy the feelings of confidence, health, vibrancy, excitement, and resolution.

Allow yourself to feel all of these emotions, and then quickly think of the color green. See the color green and imagine the room filled with green. Or, you could visualize a screen surrounding you with nothing but vibrant green. Over the next few days, whenever and wherever you see the color green, it will appear brighter, sharper, more vibrant, and more alive. It doesn't matter if it is a traffic light, a t-shirt, a sign on the highway, an advertisement, or even the leaves of a salad. The color will stand out to you, in any context. At that very moment you will bring yourself back to where you are right now; successful, encouraged, healthy, vibrant, and resolute.

Sometimes you can listen with all of your attention and other times you can listen by just experiencing the process. Either way is fine. In the coming week, because of your attention to this transformation, you will find it easy to eat slower and chew all of your food. Intuitively, you know that this is healthiest way to eat because it promotes the absorption of all of the nutrients contained in each food. As you shop each day, choose new foods with new color and textures, to add to your choices. You find this be a fun challenge and a rewarding experience. Each and every day, add a salad to lunch and dinner. Eat the salad first, filling yourself with healthy, high nutrition foods.

Although these changes seem like common sense, or may even be things that you have practiced in the past, you will find that chewing food slowly, adding new foods, and eating a salad without oil or dairy dressing before lunch and dinner, will be key factors in your success. You will know a new peace and a sense of freedom by adding to your life in order to lose weight and restore your health.

HYPNOSIS SESSION 2:

Breaking addiction and changing preferences

This hypnosis session will last about ten minutes. It is what I call a "skill building" hypnosis session. In my work with alcoholics and drug addicts, I learned that success could be experienced even by those addicted to the most powerful chemicals, by helping clients to manage any of the discomfort associated with withdrawal.

Now that you have made a significant change by adding new foods and new patterns of eating into you routine, it is time to begin cutting out foods that are loaded with chemicals or foods low in nutritional value. From this point forward, you will avoid any foods with Trans fat, enriched and refined flour, and extra sugar or salt. Some might think it would be difficult to quit eating ice cream, cake, candy, white bread, and fried or prepackaged food. However, by overcoming the physical discomfort associated with breaking the cycle of addiction to these obesogens, you will have a very easy time.

I do a lot of work with cigarette smokers to help them be successful. The biggest challenge is getting them to break the habit and refrain from smoking for three days. For people who do not use hypnosis, they find these three days to be the most difficult. However, my clients who learn and use hypnosis find that even if they do have cravings, they are able to let them disappear easily by using these techniques.

In this session, you will commit to the three day challenge to be the best you can be by breaking the physical addiction to these nutritionally deficient foods. You can eat all you want to during this time period, as long as the food choices you make are healthy. If you are hungry or have a craving, use naturally sweet foods like apples and other fruit to fill yourself with a sense of success. Eating foods that are high in fiber, like bananas, are also good at helping people to manage any physical cravings.

To begin this session, get comfortable in your chair. You have already become accustomed to the process of hypnosis, and so as you relax, focus on your breath. With each breath, relax more and more. Let any of your muscles become loose and limp, letting go of any stress. With each breath, exhale the old air and breathe in new life. It feels wonderful to make such important changes, doesn't it?

Now, continue to relax your body and mind. Anytime you notice tension in the body, let it relax and melt away. Do you notice how when you intentionally relax muscles, the tension slips away and feels like it leaves your body through the heels and into the core of the earth? All of the stress and tension you carry simply melts away. Notice how your mind has also begun to relax. Return to the imagery of yourself under a clear blue sky, on a beautiful day. Notice a single white, puffy cloud in the sky, and how it slowly and leisurely moves off towards the horizon. As it becomes smaller and smaller, there will come a point where it simply drifts off into the distance. Now both your mind and body are completely relaxed. Perfect.

I am going to count backwards from five to one. As I do, let yourself go deeper into that state of serenity that we associate with hypnosis. Each number will double the sensation of relaxation and serenity. Five, four, three, two, one....

I am going to teach you a strategy for managing withdrawal. Notice how you have created a wonderful state of serenity, calmness, and relaxation. It is a state that is the opposite of stress, tension, or discomfort. You have done this very quickly, in just a few minutes, by coming to this session. Anytime you need to in the future, you can instantly return to this state of calm. You can even do this in the midst of stress, tension, or withdrawal.

One way to accomplish this is with something that we call an anchor. An anchor is like an association. We are going to create an anchor between this feeling of serenity and comfort and a specific action. As you relax, breathe slowing, calmly, smoothly, and rhythmically. Focus on your right hand, thumb, and index finger. Without moving your arm or even your wrist, touch those fingers together for a moment. Touch your thumb and index finger together, relaxing all of the muscles in your body, except these two fingers.

Now, tense only the muscles in your index finger and thumb, pressing them together tightly. Pay attention to the calm in your mind and body and the sensation of pressing the fingers together. Now, relax. Relax your fingers like the rest of your body and breathe, in and out, becoming even more relaxed. We have now created an association between this state of calm and the action of pressing your fingers together.

Press your fingers together again. Pay attention to your feelings of confidence, relaxation, and commitment. It is almost as if the point between those two fingers is a source of energy for success. Now, relax again. Perfect.

This anchor is very simple, yet quite powerful. Anytime over the next day, week, or month, if you find yourself feeling tension, stress, or withdrawal from low-nutrition food, just touch your fingers together. When you do this, you can bring yourself back to this point of calmness, serenity, and comfort. You will notice, like the puffy white cloud that floats off into the distance or like the tension that melts through your ankles and into the core of the earth, that any cravings that cause you distress simply disappear. They drift from your awareness and are replaced with an instant sense of calm and comfort.

You can do this anytime, without even closing your eyes and without losing focus on the tasks before you. You will benefit from this simple exercise by noticing that cravings pass quickly and by being aware of your new knowledge. You know that by giving into cravings, you only restart the cycle of addiction. This is something that you now have the power to give up by easily passing up any of the old choices that have contributed to your weight or poor health. Immediately, upon touching your fingers together, you will replace any old patters with healthy snacks, or even the ability to enjoy a normal feeling of hunger, rather than the toxic hunger that old patterns used to bring about.

You have made much progress and this short session has been designed to give you a specific skill. Take another moment or two to enjoy this progress and to recognize that something as simple as touching your fingers together can be an anchor that helps to guide you to a new chapter in life.

(Silence)

It is time to reorient to the room around you. Pay attention to your breathing, the air around you, and the feeling of sitting in the chair. Before you open your eyes, take in a deep breath and feel the power of health and your ability to control each and every sensation you experience. Take in another deep breath, feeling enthusiastic and aware, almost ready to open the eyes. Now, stretch out any muscles that need to be stretched and open the eyes when you are ready. You feel alert, oriented, and ready to enjoy the rest of the day.

HYPNOSIS SESSION 3:

Creating healthy habits, increasing physical activity, and enhancing self-esteem

In this session, we will focus on suggestions for healthy habits, increasing physical activity, and on your self-perceptions. You have learned a lot and have already experienced change that is helping you to reach your goals.

The induction I have chosen to guide you into hypnosis will help you to focus on your ability to shift your awareness to anything you choose. This will help you to implement those skills when captivated by an unpleasant emotion, feeling toxic hunger, or even in simply shifting your mood when it needs to be realigned. It might even help you to tune out the distractions in our busy world that sometimes just seem to add to the stress of life.

Again, it does not matter if you go into a deep and profound hypnotic state, only experiencing this process, or remain in a light trance, listening to each word. What matters is that you have decided to continue on this pathway of success.

Induction

Countdown Deepener

Some people fear weight gain, but as you have already experienced through hypnosis, you have the ability to control your body. You have the ability to relax, slow down your heart rate, and breathe slow, smooth, and rhythmic. You also have the ability to control your diet and increase your daily activities.

Although it is true that your body needs more physical activity to burn calories, you find that this is easy to accomplish. It is easy to accomplish because your body is now energized by oxygen, clean air, and restful sleep. It is not difficult for you to increase your activity level, go for a walk, or even go to the gym. Now, you have the energy and stamina to do these things. In the mornings, you will wake up refreshed and energetic, ready to take on the challenges of the day.

One of these challenges will be to exercise and burn calories through increased activities. It is not a difficult challenge to master, because deep within you is the desire to care for your body. You also know that you have total control over your body.

For some reason, I am always drawn to talk shows and TV interviews with people who have lost a tremendous amount of weight. Some of them are famous and some are not. What I find interesting is that almost all of these successful people, whether they used hypnosis, medication, or even surgeries, all have one thing in common. They have increased their daily activity level. Successful people like Jared from Subway, Richard Simmons, and Al Roker, all take regular walks. Some of these people have even attributed their incredible weight loss to walking, alone.

In the end, I think Jared's success came primarily from walking to subway, rather the food choices he made. Walking is the most affordable and easiest exercise to implement. You are already doing it each day. Simply add steps each day. Take more steps today than yesterday, more steps tomorrow, and even more steps the next day. This will help you to quickly and easily increase your success, your fitness, and your health.

You have already completed previous hypnosis sessions, so I know that you are sincerely motivated to continue your success. Go to any sporting goods store, or even a large general store that sells sporting goods, and purchase a pedometer. This will be a tremendous investment in your future, yet will cost less than fifteen dollars. By getting a pedometer, which is a device that attaches to your clothing and counts your steps, you can accurately measure your steps and continue to reach your goal of walking more steps each day.

Losing weight and keeping it off is very important to you. From this point forward, you will be able to see the weight you want to lose melt off your body. You will find that losing two to four pounds a week is an easily attainable goal. You will develop new eating habits that bring you happiness and satisfaction.

In the past, you ate more than your body needed for its energy requirements. From this point forward, until your goals are reached, you will eat slightly less than what your body requires.

After reaching your goals, you will find yourself eating exactly the amount your body needs. Let your body tell you how much nutrition it needs. The body is intuitive, and it will be easy for you to listen to it. Feed yourself only what you need for energy and health and then simply stop.

Relax into a deeper state of hypnosis and let these suggestions begin to take hold in your mind. You no longer eat fast. Instead, you will slowly eat your food, allowing your body to feel fuller and more satisfied with each bite. You will find that eating is no longer a task, but an experience like watching snow falling. It is refreshing and peaceful. The anxieties you have about eating are gone. From this point forward, you can eat with confidence, knowing that you are choosing healthy foods and nutrients. You will choose portions that are appropriate and no longer have the desire to "clean your plate". You will eat until you are satisfied. Then, you will simply stop and choose not to eat anymore.

Relax. Let your mind wander as you enjoy peace and tranquility. You are giving up old ideas and creating new associations with food. From this point forward, you will feel that food meets your nutritional needs and you will cease seeing food as an item of comfort in difficult times. Instead, during those difficult times you will draw upon your ability to concentrate and focus. You will create happy and positive images in order to overcome negative emotions. You will envision yourself in a circle of satisfaction, enjoying life as a thinner and healthier person.

From this point forward, you will give up old ideas and associations. You can see bread as a delicious food on its own, without the need for jellies and butter. Salads will be refreshing on their own and will not need the embellishment of condiments to become satisfactory.

Imagine that a blanket of snow has fallen, covering the ground. It is a deep snow, but as the daylight comes, it begins to shrink away. From this point forward, the portions of food that you serve yourself will also begin to shrink.

As you picture the snow melting away in the sun, imagine the pounds melting from your body.

Losing weight really is this easy. You are feeling refreshed with healthy food choices and you enjoy whole grain breads, lean protein, and leafy vegetables. This nutritional fare will give you a sense of renewed energy, enabling you to exercise more.

At first, you will simply walk each day. Then, you will move on to higher levels of physical activity, with each pound that is lost. Succeeding each week will reinforce your desire to experience more success. The reward you will give yourself is permission to continue losing weight, until you reach your goal.

Imagine yourself three to six months from now, creating a mental picture of how good you feel when the goal you have set becomes a reality. In your mind's eye, see yourself happy, free, healthy, energetic, thin, attractive, and abundantly hopeful. From this point forward, you will see food as a tool to assist you in caring for your body. You will see buffets as an opportunity to make healthy choices, in the correct portions.

From this point forward, you will see healthy foods as something you enjoy. Your automatic pattern will be to sit down while eating and to eating your food slowly. You will choose smaller portions of food and feel full and satisfied after just a few bites. You will be able to visualize pounds melting from your body, just as the springtime sun melts the piles of snow that have fallen in the night. From this point forward, you will use your renewed energy to engage in meaningful activities that expend energy and burn calories.

HYPNOSIS SESSION 4:

Relapse prevention, motivation, and continued success

There is no doubt you have benefitted from the previous sessions and have already begun to feel the profound changes within you. This fourth session is a short session, designed to give you the tools for relapse prevention. It will also promote continued motivation towards success.

This session also provides positive affirmation exercises. This technique integrates very well with hypnosis. Positive affirmation is successful because self-talk changes our internal dialog and can reprogram a lifetime of self-defeating messages with the truth. The truth is that you are able to create your success, restore your body, and be physically fit.

By now, you are very familiar with the process of hypnosis, so get comfortable in your chair. Begin by focusing on your breathing and relax more with each breath. Scan your body. Anywhere you are experiencing any remaining tension, let that tension melt away. Let it disappear from your body, draining down, down, all the way down. Let it leave your body through the soles of your feet. Let that energy of tension be consumed by the core of the earth, leaving you deeply relaxed.

Although you know you could open your eyes or move your body, you will find it much easier to relax deeply. Let your muscles be heavy and your body be comfortable. Focus your attention on your breath. Notice how it has become smooth and rhythmic. Your heartbeat is calm and regular.

I am going to count backwards now. Five, four, three, two, one. Perfect.

You have made many changes by adding new things to your life and by reducing those things that were not helpful to you. You have found that the benefit of these changes is increased energy, a slimmer body, and a wonderful feeling of health.

It is now time to ratify this commitment that you have already taken action on and remove any possibility of returning to unhealthy patterns of eating. This moment is a special time to make a commitment to yourself to be good to your body, good to your mind, and good to your spirit by making these changes permanent. What you have embarked on is far different than a diet. Rather, it is a permanent change that treats your body exactly the way nature intended for your body to be treated.

Chances are that in your city there are places that you drive past that were once empty parcels of ground. Years later, people have moved and situations and changed. Now, these empty parcels have been replaced with vibrant signs of life, commerce, and human activity. You also have a vibrant new way of living, with new places to shop, new ways of seeing the world around you, and new feelings of health. When you drive by these places, it is clear that they will never return to the empty parcels of ground that they once were. They will always be vibrant centers of activity and life. The old has passed away. You have entered a new chapter of life. Without missing the past, only accepting what it once was, your new habits and new patterns are the new "you". These new habits bring health, vitality, and success.

As you shed pounds, feel energetic, sleep better, and even save money, you intuitively prefer this new manner of living. You choose to grow in your knowledge of nutritional eating, reading books, and viewing websites that will help you to continue to expand beyond the knowledge of these sessions.

It is remarkable how you still experience the color green as being sharper, brighter, crisper, and clearer. You notice it more often, too. It brings with it a sense of empowerment and success. It is also amazing how returning to a point of decision, serenity, or success, can easily be accomplished by touching the fingers together. These things you have learned and practiced over the past few weeks will remain a part of your lifestyle, bringing a permanent sense of well-being in every aspect of life.

Affirmations are a wonderful part of a healthy lifestyle. We only act on what we believe. Therefore, telling yourself the truth is important to hear and it contributes to adapting new patterns of behavior. As you relax, I will share some affirmations with you. You can repeat these affirmations after I do, either silently or out loud, making them your own words and letting them become part of your life. The first three affirmations are about you as a person. The next three focus on your behavior. Finally, the last three focus on your future.

Repeat after me:

1. I am worthy of caring for myself.
2. I am a healthy person.
3. I am a secure and significant.

Now, let's look at three affirmations relating to your behavior:

1. I choose foods that are high in nutritional value.
2. I look for ways to increase my activity each day.
3. I care for myself by planning my meals in advance.

Now, let's focus on the future:

1. I create health, each and every day.
2. I am able to create my own vision.
3. I am becoming who I want to be, each and every day.

At this point, you have experienced a lot of change. You can take time for yourself each day to practice setting goals, focusing your energy, and experiencing success. You can congratulate yourself for doing very well and making so many changes. It is good to review these positive affirmations and make them a part of your lifestyle. You can even create your own affirmations.

The HYPNOSIS CONVENTION for those Passionate about Helping Other People… Clinical Hypnosis Training for Caring Professionals

(ICBCH Continuing Education Hours Provided)

ALL THREE DAYS, ALL SPEAKERS, ONE LOW REGISTRATION RATE!

Karen Hand and Kelley T. Woods
with Keynote by Jason Linette

DAY ONE – All Day Seminar

One Day Intensive "How to Create Hypnosis Workshops for the Public" is included in your 3-day registration!

MONDAY, FEBRUARY 17 | 9:00AM-5:00PM

Karen Hand and Kelley T. Woods are going to help you create outstanding hypnosis workshops and seminars for the public. If you have ever wondered how to use hypnosis in group settings to create interest and referrals to your practice, they have the answers. You will learn what seminars people want to attend, and how to structure and create programs that sell. This is perhaps one of the single best skills you can learn if you want to build a thriving private practice with lots of community referrals. Be a part of this event!

---

25 Expert Level Speakers Sharing the Exact Tools They Use to Create Therapeutic Success

Two full days packed with approved continuing education that will change your client outcomes
TUESDAY AND WEDNESDAY, FEBRUARY 18-19, 2020 | 8AM-6PM EACH DAY
We have hand-picked the highest rated speakers, with the most practical ideas and innovative approaches. We want you to leave this conference not only having had a great time but also maximizing your potential as a passionate hypnotherapist. We record everything, but the video is ONLY available to those who pre-register for the conference. This way, even though you have to make a choice as to which room to attend, you still get them all a few weeks after the conference!

THE NEXT STEP!

Now that you have saved your seat, get your hotel reservations! The Orleans is offering the first 100 to book room nights a special discount (plus mandatory resort fee). The Orleans Hotel and Casino is a landmark hotel in Las Vegas. It is conveniently located near the south end of Las Vegas Blvd. but just off the strip at 4500 W Tropicana Ave in Las Vegas, Nevada. All travel, lodging and meals expenses are the responsibility of attendee and are not included in conference registration/tuition fees.

Questions? Call (702) 418-3332 to Register by Phone or visit HPTI.org to Register Online